backstage pass

Backstage at a
NEWSCAST

Barbara A. Somervill

HIGH
interest
books

Children's Press®
A Division of Scholastic Inc.
New York / Toronto / London / Auckland / Sydney
Mexico City / New Delhi / Hong Kong
Danbury, Connecticut

The author thanks Allison Standard, Lee Brown, Michelle Willis, and the WYFF News Team in Greenville, South Carolina, for their assistance with this book.

Thanks to the Intensive Television News Production Program of the Film, Video, and Broadcasting Department, New York University School of Continuing and Professional Studies

To Nanny

Book Design: Daniel Hosek and Christopher Logan
Contributing Editor: Matthew Pitt
Photo Credits: Cover, p. 34 © ABC News/Everett Collection; pp. 4, 33 © Joseph Sohm/ChromoSohm Inc./Corbis; pp. 6–7 © Annie Griffiths Belt/Corbis; p. 8 © AFP/Corbis; p. 11 © David Woo/TimePix; pp. 12, 15 © Bettmann/Corbis; pp. 16, 19, 27, 29, 30, 41 Cindy Reiman; p. 20 © Roger Ressmeyer/Corbis; p. 24 © Reuters NewMedia Inc./Corbis; p. 36 © Mitchell Gerber/Corbis; p. 39 © Kim Steele/Getty Images

Library of Congress Cataloging-in-Publication Data

Somervill, Barbara A., 1948–
    Backstage at a newscast / Barbara A. Somervill.
    p. cm. — (Backstage pass)
    Includes index.
    ISBN 0-516-24326-8 (lib. bdg.) — ISBN 0-516-24388-8 (pbk.)
    1. Television broadcasting of news—Juvenile literature. I. Title.
    II. Series.

PN4784.T4 S66 2003
070.1'95—dc21

                                        2002010693

CONTENTS

Whether they are covering the activities of news-making personalities or hurricanes in Florida, TV journalists have to get close to their subjects to bring you the story.

Introduction

7:45 A.M. The morning news meeting for Florida TV station WZIP Channel 5 gets underway. The staff begins to toss around story ideas for the five o'clock evening newscast. Suddenly, Chuck Malone, the station's meteorologist, rushes into the room. Pointing to a report in his hand, he announces, "There's a huge hurricane over the Atlantic. It's already destroyed a few homes in the Caribbean. Now it's headed our way."

Weather reports are usually a small part of a TV newscast. A destructive hurricane, however, is big news. It often becomes the newscast's lead story.

The news director checks her wristwatch. "How much time before it hits us?"

Malone glances over his notes. "We've got a couple of hours—if we're lucky."

There's no time to waste. Immediately, three reporters are sent to different locations to cover the hurricane's arrival. They travel with camera crews, packing first aid kits and food supplies into their vans. Portable electric generators are also brought

along, in case the region's power supply goes
down. The reporters slip into hip boots. These
boots will keep them dry in case of flash flooding.
They also strap on ankle weights. These will prevent
them from being blown over by howling winds.

The hurricane finally hits. Winds gust to 120
miles (193.1 kilometers) an hour. Tides surge 15
feet (4.6 meters) high. Over the next few hours,
WZIP's viewers will depend on Channel 5's newscasts to track the storm's progress. The station's

reporters must keep their audience informed. Chuck Malone airs regular reports. He describes up-to-the-minute weather conditions. He predicts which way the hurricane is headed. Suddenly, WZIP switches to a live, on-location feed: "Good afternoon, I'm Lily Simon, reporting from Jacksonville. Just moments ago, Hurricane Jake furiously tore through this community...."

Citizens of coastal communities, such as this one, rely on TV reporters to warn them of approaching storms.

Even though some newscasters had been sent anthrax-tainted mail, it was their duty to sort through the rumors and report the facts.

CHAPTER ONE

A Signal for Change

In the fall of 2001, several Americans mysteriously contracted a deadly disease called anthrax. Traces of the germs that cause the disease were found on letters and envelopes that were delivered to them. TV stations sprang into action to get to the bottom of this frightening situation. News anchors and reporters tried to cover every angle of the story: Can anthrax be treated? How did the germs get on the letters and envelopes? Should American citizens stop opening their mail?

The anthrax story was a difficult one to cover. New scares and hoaxes surfaced every day. Newsrooms had to make sure they were reporting facts, not spreading rumors. Making matters even worse, many letters with anthrax germs had been mailed to TV stations! Now, anchors were not simply reporting the news. Suddenly, they were the subjects of the news.

It was critical that TV newsrooms continued to broadcast. While radio announcers might be able to describe the symptoms of anthrax, TV newscasters could do much more. They could show photos of what anthrax germs look like. They could also show the tainted letters and envelopes. They could even broadcast photographs of those suspected of mailing the deadly letters. This frightening story, however, is just one fascinating event in the long, rich history of TV news broadcasting.

THE FIRST SIGNALS

TV programs in the United States began to be broadcast in 1930. On July 30 of that year, the National Broadcasting Company (NBC) opened a TV station. The Columbia Broadcasting System (CBS) started its first station the following year. In 1938, CBS's *World News Roundup* became the first major TV news show. Most people, however, still tuned in to radios for the day's news. TV sets were expensive and not yet common in households.

After World War II, television took off. Fascination for this new technology grew.

Television could transmit information across thousands of miles in an instant. Unlike radio, television could broadcast pictures *and* words. TV stations beamed world events into homes everywhere. People could now see the news that made history. In 1963, horrified viewers watched footage of the shooting of President John F. Kennedy. Six years later, 90 percent of TV viewers in the United States witnessed a unique, live show. What a show it was!

When President John F. Kennedy was assassinated, the United States went into a deep state of mourning. For many Americans, images of the shooting would haunt them for years. This photo is from the movie *JFK*, a retelling of the assassination.

Audiences stared in disbelief as *Apollo XI* made its lunar landing. They shared astronaut Neil Armstrong's thrill as he took mankind's first steps on the Moon.

THE WAY IT WAS

Many early TV journalists got their start on radio. There, they sharpened their reporting skills by covering tough assignments. Many of these journalists went on to become stars on television. The first TV

Today's TV journalists try to shape their own personal style. Often, though, their style is influenced by watching Edward R. Murrow (left) and Walter Cronkite (center), two early pioneers of TV broadcasting.

Trade Secret

Murrow didn't think being a strong broadcaster took much. "All you have to do is love the news," he insisted. Murrow certainly proved he loved it. During his twenty-five-year career, he made more than 5,000 broadcasts!

news celebrities were Edward R. Murrow and Walter Cronkite.

Murrow broadcasted radio reports covering World War II action from London, England. After the war, he made the move to TV news reporting. Murrow hosted popular programs such as *See It Now* and *Person to Person*. Murrow made a lasting impression on how news was reported.

Cronkite began his news career with the United Press, in 1939. The United Press provides stories for newspapers, radio, and television. In 1950, Cronkite joined CBS. He was immediately put to work hosting shows and covering presidential debates. In 1962, he became the anchor on the CBS evening news program. Viewers came to rely on Cronkite's accurate reporting. They knew he would fully and fairly sum up the day's major events. He signed off each newscast with the phrase, "That's the way it was."

Millions of Americans valued Cronkite's wisdom and insight—and American politicians knew this. In the late 1960s, Cronkite criticized President Lyndon B. Johnson's decision to keep fighting the Vietnam War. President Johnson was watching Cronkite's broadcast that day. After hearing the anchorman's opinion, Johnson turned to an aide. "If I've lost Cronkite," he said, "I've lost Middle America."

NOW, MORE THAN EVER

Important events can take place anywhere, and at any time. Many Americans want to see and hear these events the instant they happen. To meet this demand, Ted Turner founded the Cable News Network (CNN) on June 1, 1980. CNN reports news 24 hours a day. CNN news correspondents report from almost every country in the world. World leaders often tune into CNN for late-breaking news.

When Americans were taken hostage in Iran in 1979, TV viewers in the United States wanted information about the situation. The news program *Nightline* got it's start by giving information to anxious Americans about the hostages' terrifying plight.

People have proven to have large appetites for many different forms of news. Some want to see the latest sports highlights. The cable network ESPN was created for them. Others want to watch the U.S. government in action on the Cable Satellite Public Affairs Network. You probably know this network simply as C-SPAN.

The news team at WZIP zips into action the moment their morning meeting gets underway.

CHAPTER TWO

What's the Story?

8:00 A.M. Members of WZIP's news team arrive at the station. For the next 10 hours, WZIP's newsroom will be bustling with action. Producers will plan schedules. The assignment editor will send crews out to follow tips on breaking news. Reporters will frantically write stories. Directors will review scripts and videos for broadcasts. In the afternoon, the anchors will arrive. They'll go through the rundown of the evening newscast. They'll practice announcing the stories. Meanwhile, makeup artists and wardrobe planners will make sure the anchors look perfect for the broadcast. The team must fill three half-hour news programs that air at 5:00, 5:30, and 6:00 P.M. It might take two dozen people to put together each half-hour show.

LEADING OFF

News producers decide which lead stories will begin each show. Choosing the right lead story is an important part of planning a newscast. A good lead draws in viewers. If a lead isn't compelling, audiences may switch off their TV sets!

Some stations choose lead stories based on how thrilling the news is. These stations place importance on crimes and serious accidents. Such stations might lead with a story about a tiger escaping from a zoo. Meanwhile, another station might lead with a story about the local high school choir singing for the U.S. president.

Tonight's lead story is easy to pick. Two days ago, several ill manatees were discovered along the Florida coastline. Three others were found dead in the area. No one is sure why these creatures are straying so far from their habitat. The story has been nicknamed "The Manatee Mystery."

Once leads are chosen, producers divide up the remaining stories. Each half-hour newscast needs eight to ten general news stories. They also require two weather pieces and about six sports reports. Some reports will run as short as 20 seconds. Others may run for as long as 6 minutes. Reporters, producers, and editors research and write these stories.

This WZIP anchor practices reading her scripts before the 5:00 P.M. broadcast. She must read her reports with a perfect blend of drama and clarity.

A director then reviews the script of each story before it airs.

An anchorperson opens the newscast and introduces stories. Many anchors also write and present reports. For example, if an anchor is interested in health and medicine, he or she may write all stories related to these topics.

"You're Live!"

Newscast reports can either be live or taped. There's a big difference between the two. Taped reports are easily edited to fix any mistakes. Live reports can cause a lot of tension in the newsroom. Broadcasters and camera crews get only one chance to get a live report right.

Many newscasts feature coanchors who report the news. It's crucial that coanchors respect and get along with one another. To perfect their smooth delivery, coanchors often practice their scripts together.

Trade Secret

Some stories combine taped and live segments. They're known as donuts. A donut, for example, might open with a live shot of the reporter. Later in the story, part of an interview taped earlier that day may be shown.

So why go live? Live stories present the freshest news. Usually, live reports are favored when a story is still unfolding. It's one thing to tape a speech by the mayor for a later broadcast. That's a scheduled news event. When the mayor is finished talking, the story is over. On the other hand, what if police officers are involved in a high-speed car chase with a bank robber? If the news station waits to air an edited tape of this incident, the story may be old news by broadcast time. Audiences expect to see dramatic events, such as a police chase, the moment they occur.

BUILDING A SCHEDULE

Newscasts follow a strict schedule. As the day unfolds, the newscast schedule begins to fill up.

Every second of a broadcast must be mapped out—including time for the station's theme song and commercials! A schedule lists the title of each story and that story's length. It also indicates when each story should appear in the broadcast, and which anchor will introduce it.

News producers direct each newscast. At stations with newscasts at 5:00, 5:30, and 6:00 P.M., each show has a different producer. Producers plan the schedule and run the actual show. They must make sure their show starts and ends on time. Throughout the broadcast, they track how long each segment runs. If the show is running too long, a report can be dropped to gain needed seconds.

Our Top Story Tonight

Newscast producers choose stories that interest their viewers. Good news items can have local, regional, national, or international slants. The audience needs to relate to every story in some way.

The station's staff of reporters covers the local and regional stories. They may also cover beats. Beats are areas of local interest in which a reporter becomes an expert. Local beats include crime, education, and community service. Reporters use a beat system to find news and develop more in-depth stories. They may build strong ties to the people on their beat.

National and international stories usually come from news services. These include the Associated Press (AP) and United Press International (UPI). Examples of national news that would interest local viewers might include a story about the latest presidential election or a tax bill being voted on by the U.S. Congress.

WZIP's producer looks over the schedule. It seems to be shaping up well. The newsroom seems fairly calm. In fact, the newscast's producer wonders if it's a bit *too* calm....

As workers scramble at the site of a train wreck, TV reporters scramble too. They try to find out important details that their viewers want to know, such as the cause of the accident or how many people were hurt.

CHAPTER THREE

Breaking News

THIS JUST IN

Just 90 minutes before the 5:00 P.M. newscast, a citizen calls the station with a stunning tip: A passenger train has crashed just outside his home.

The assignment editor quickly pulls a reporter off a story about littering in public parks. After all, litter is an everyday problem. A train wreck is major news.

Assignment editors are responsible for checking on tips provided by citizens. People often call newsrooms or send tips by E-mail. Also, assignment editors listen to police and fire department scanners to pick up breaking news. They send reporters and crews out to get stories. They keep track of the people and equipment that could be helpful in gathering each story's details.

Using the station's helicopter, the reporter and the camera crew fly to the accident site. They will broadcast via remote feed to the station. Now, time becomes a factor. How long will they take to reach the site? Will the story be ready to lead the 5:00 P.M. news?

The reporter and the camera crew have a plan of action. At the train wreck, the reporter will question members of the police and fire departments. He'll locate bystanders who witnessed the wreck and interview them. His producer has told him that his report needs to fill 1 minute and 45 seconds, or 1:45, of the newscast.

Meanwhile, the camera crew will be busy shooting footage of the derailed train. They'll film the reporter telling the story and conducting interviews. A camera crew might shoot 20 or 30 minutes of film just to make a 1:45 piece.

When they return to WZIP, everyone will be in for more hard work. They will try to put together a report for the 5:00 P.M. broadcast. Scenes from the video, called the B-roll, will be chosen. The reporter will add graphics—printed words or pictures—to the film. The reporter may also develop a tease. A tease is a brief piece aired during the

This video editor is adding an important graphic that will appear on viewers' TV screens during the WZIP broadcast. She places the phone number that families of the train passengers can call to learn more about the accident.

newscast or during commercial breaks. Teases urge viewers to watch the complete report. The report, graphics, film, and tease make up a package.

Decision Time

All of this will take time—a luxury the station doesn't have. The news producer looks at the clock. The newscast is 5 minutes from airing.

She must decide which lead to run with. The train wreck is a huge story. The helicopter, however, hasn't landed at the scene yet. Also, "The Manatee Mystery" has captivated audiences over the last two days. Will viewers flip to another station if WZIP doesn't lead with it?

The producer decides to lead with the late-breaking story. While "The Manatee Mystery" is a big story, nothing newsworthy has happened with the story today. Unfortunately, no new clues have emerged. The producer decides to open her newscast with live images of the wreck, taken from the hovering chopper. Later in the broadcast, once her remote crew lands, she'll cut to their live report.

ON LOCATION

Today's WZIP newscast also features remote feeds from the state fair. Since this was a planned event, the crew isn't as tense as the one covering the train wreck. Still, putting this story together is difficult work. The crew had to pack a full set of equipment when they left for the fair site at 10:00 A.M. today. They knew they wouldn't be able to return to the station for equipment such as batteries or electric cable. There are two ways to send TV signals from remote places. If the location is close, a direct signal is sent by microwave. For longer distances, signals are beamed off satellites.

From WZIP's control booth, skilled technicians are calling the shots. They decide, minute-by-minute, which anchors and which camera angles viewers will be seeing as they watch the newscast.

TIME TO ROLL

The anchor freshens up her makeup. She takes a sip of water. Then she quickly checks the schedule of tonight's show. Her coanchor reminds her that the audience still thinks the lead story will involve "The Manatee Mystery." The producer counts down, "We're live in five, four, three, two...."

With only half an hour to present so many stories, the key to a smooth newscast is preparation. In this photo, a technician assists the anchors with their clip-on microphones.

"Good evening, this is Maggie Jacks. Welcome to News at Five on Five. We'll be following up on 'The Manatee Mystery' later in this broadcast. Our top story tonight involves a train wreck on the city's East Side. Let's go now to our Chopper Five helicopter. A camera crew is bringing you live footage of the wreck."

The producer speaks to Maggie Jacks through a headset. From a control booth in the studio, the producer tells Jacks to slow down her reading. The helicopter needs a few seconds to get into position. That way, they'll get the clearest shot of the derailed train.

Behind the Lens

The most important player of all is watching WZIP's newscast unfold from an office at the Channel 5 station. The news director controls the entire newsroom. This person plans the annual budget for producing the news. A news director hires people and purchases new equipment. He or she also reviews news items to make sure they are well written and well produced.

How Does It Rate?

After the newscast, WZIP's news director anxiously studies the show's ratings. Ratings tell how many viewers watched the broadcast. The more viewers a show gets, the higher the ratings. The higher the ratings, the more the station can charge advertisers for commercial time.

More ad money creates better opportunities for the news team. The extra money might go toward hiring more reporters. It might allow the news director to buy better camera equipment or even a new helicopter.

Trade Secret

About one in four news directors are women. Fewer than one in ten news directors belong to a minority group.

News choppers provide their audiences with an "eye-in-the-sky" viewpoint of dangerous events. News stations are able to purchase helicopters with money paid to them by advertisers.

TV news anchor Peter Jennings spends countless hours reviewing notes and rehearsing scripts before important broadcasts, such as this presidential convention.

CHAPTER FOUR

Get on Air!

Can you picture yourself working in a newsroom? What position do you think would suit you best? On camera? How about behind the lens, capturing the unforgettable images that make up major news events? Or can you see yourself running the entire newscast?

ANCHOR YOUR DREAM

Many people dream of becoming TV announcers. Anchors seem to lead glamorous lives. Like everyone else in the newsroom, though, anchors put in long hours. Most local news anchors arrive at the station at around 2:00 P.M. for a 5:00 P.M. show. Before broadcasts, they must review the schedule, write scripts, and polish their reading. Many anchors announce three broadcasts between 5:00 and 11:00 P.M. Often, they do not head home until midnight.

News announcers must build solid presentation skills. They speak slowly and clearly. They avoid

National news anchors may get the opportunity to interview some of the world's most powerful men and women. Paula Zahn has interviewed four U.S. presidents, Cuban president Fidel Castro, and Queen Noor of Jordan.

saying "um," "you know," or "like." They practice pronouncing difficult words, such as the names of people and places. Announcers must know their subjects. Viewers expect to trust TV anchors to learn the facts about the day's news.

A TV anchor is the "face" of both the news station and the town or city in which the station is located. To prove their commitment to the town, anchors often work on community-service projects. They may also attend major public events and help local charities. These efforts help anchors develop a bond of trust and loyalty with their viewers.

SPORTS AND WEATHER

Sports and weather anchors normally report later in a newscast. During special occasions, though, they may see their roles expanded. Suppose the local college basketball team has made it into the Final Four NCAA Basketball Championship. In this case, the sportscaster would probably lead off the broadcast.

A local sportscaster's job may be very different from a sportscaster who broadcasts on a network. An ESPN anchor may specialize in one sport. A local sportscaster must report on all sports, national and regional. They must be able to cover the high school volleyball squad as well as the major league baseball action.

Forecasting the weather has become a high-tech job. Radar, computer models, and long-term forecasts have replaced gazing at the clouds. National weather services provide everything from satellite pictures of storms to local wind conditions. News stations expect weather anchors to have degrees in meteorology. Weather anchors are also expected to understand all aspects of local weather. For instance, a meteorologist in Nebraska would need to understand how a long drought could damage farm crops.

IT'S YOUR TURN

If you want a career in TV journalism, start following your dream now. Most high schools publish a newspaper. Usually, a teacher runs the paper and assigns students to write the stories. Some schools even provide classes and equipment for student

ON THE WEB

Each news station wants to be a viewer's complete news source. To achieve this, many stations offer their own Web sites. These sites often provide extra information. For instance, South Carolina's WYFF Web site offers many features. Their Money page provides plenty of articles that help viewers make smart purchasing decisions. Also, links connect Web surfers to *Smart Money* and *Business Week* magazines.

broadcasts. If you have the opportunity, start a news-cast at school. Here are some tips to get you started:

- Write news articles about current sports and events. Make sure you've reported on the who, what, when, where, why, and how of each event.
- Report on important school policy changes, such as dress code or detention.
- Use simple, clear language and short sentences.

It takes a lot of effort to predict the path of Mother Nature. Most meteorologists must receive years of training before a news station will hire them to make forecasts. In this photo, the station's meteorologists review a series of weather maps just before air time.

• Practice reading in front of a camera. Speak directly to the camera as if it were a friend. It's important to keep eye contact with your viewers.

Whether they work for newspapers or TV stations, reporters need to develop strong writing and interviewing skills. They must do their own research and find the right facts. Here are some tips for a successful interview:

• Learn about your person and topic ahead of time.
• Make a list of thoughtful questions to ask.
• Avoid questions that get "yes" or "no" answers.
• Create a relaxing atmosphere.

A TV newsroom is a hustling, bustling workplace. The hours are grueling and long. The work, however, is so exciting and rewarding that few workers at the station notice. Like Edward R. Murrow, they just "love the news," and so will you.

THAT'S ALL THE
►NEWS WE HAVE
FOR YOU TONIGHT.
I'M

AND I'M

To become a member of a city or town's TV newsroom, you have to channel your energy into hard work and dedication.

NEW WORDS

anchorperson the main person who reports the news on a TV news show

assignment the story that a reporter researches and reports about

beat a general area of interest assigned to a reporter

B-roll the video portion of a report

correspondent someone who reports for television, radio, or newspapers about a special subject or place

feed the connection between a remote location and the TV station

hoaxes tricks or practical jokes

lead the first story of each newscast

lunar to do with the moon

meteorologist a scientist who studies Earth's atmosphere, climate, and weather

microwave a wave that can pass through solid objects, and is used to send messages over long distances

network a group of television stations that are connected to each other

news director the manager of a news team

producer the person who plans and runs a news program

remote far away, or distant

rundown the schedule of a newscast

tease a small section of a news report meant to hook viewers into watching the entire broadcast

FOR FURTHER READING

Boraas, Tracey. *TV Reporters*. Mankato, MN: Capstone Press, 1999.

Chambers, Catherine. *Television*. Portsmouth, NH: Heinemann Library, 2001.

Koral, April. *In the Newsroom*. Danbury, CT: Franklin Watts, 1997.

Organizations
Radio-Television News Directors Association
1600 K Street NW, Suite 700
Washington, DC 20006-2838
(202) 659-6510
www.rtnda.org

American Sportscasters Association
225 Broadway, Suite 2030
New York, NY 10007-3722
(212) 227-8080
www.americansportscasters.com

Minorities in Broadcasting
P. O. Box 1475
Santa Clarita, CA 91386-1475
(661) 250-0080

RESOURCES

Web Sites
Interactive News Game
www.pbs.org/wnet/insidelocalnews/newscast.html
On this site, you will learn about one of the hardest jobs in broadcasting as you play the assignment editor for a local news show.

Broadcast Education Association
www.beaweb.org
This Web site provides information on scholarships and grants available to future journalists.

Public Broadcasting System
www.pbs.org/neighborhoods/news/
This site is an excellent resource for national and international news.

CNN.com
www.cnn.com
Get great insights into how a national-level news show is put together on this site.

The Rundown
www.tvrundown.com
This on-line magazine covers everything from TV journalism education to available jobs in the field.

INDEX

About the Author

Barbara A. Somervill sees every project she undertakes as an opportunity to learn new information. She writes books for children, video scripts, magazine articles, and textbooks. Barbara was raised and educated in New York. She has also lived in Canada, Australia, California, and South Carolina. She is an avid reader and traveler, and enjoys movies and live theater.